IN MEMORIAM
NORMAN O. BROWN

Edited by Jerome Neu

New Pacific Press
Santa Cruz, California
2005

Published and distributed in the United States by
New Pacific Press
204 Locust Street
Santa Cruz, CA 95060

www.literaryguillotine.com/npp/npphome.html

Copyright © 2005 by New Pacific Press

All rights reserved. No part of this book may be reproduced in any form without permission from the publisher.

First published 2005

10 9 8 7 6 5 4 3 2 1

New Pacific Press was established in 2003 as a "Hey, we'll at least break even" alternative to the commercial, homogeneous publications that currently dominate the publishing industry. New Pacific Press does not believe that it necessarily serves the public interest to operate a not-for-profit enterprise, but rather that there is both value and viability in publishing small, innovative, educational and culturally significant works that the mainstream may consider small potatoes. Our planned publications will be primarily socio-political, economic, cultural studies; they will be scholarly, personal, poetic, mixed-media presentations that reflect the multiplicity of cultural work being done in the greater Bay Area and throughout the Pacific Rim(s).

Book design by Petra Serafim
Set in FF Scala, FF Scala Sans and Adobe Sabon

Cover photo by Thomas N. Brown

ISBN 09712546-1-3

Printed in Canada by Hemlock Printers Ltd.

Contents

Preface   v

Memoirs
Norman O. Brown   3

In Memoriam: Norman O. Brown
*A Ceremony at the University of California, Santa Cruz
October 19, 2002*

UCSC Faculty

Jerome Neu   39
   Humanities

James Clifford   45
   History of Consciousness

Christopher Connery   51
   Literature

Nathaniel Mackey   56
   Literature

Robert Meister   65
   Politics

Helene Moglen   72
   Literature

Hayden White   79
   History of Consciousness, emeritus

Other Friends of Nobby

Carl E. Schorske   83
Princeton University, History, emeritus

Rebecca Herzig   88
Bates College, Women and Gender Studies

Jay Cantor   91
Tufts University, English

Family

Stephen R. Brown   97
Eldest Son

Preface

A memorial service in honor of Norman O. Brown was held at the University of California, Santa Cruz on October 19, 2002. What follows are the invited statements that were made on that occasion. The statements are mainly from colleagues who were close to Nobby during his years at Santa Cruz, and they are here presented basically in the order they were made, and largely unchanged. (There is also one submission that came later.) The floor was also opened, Quaker Meeting style, for others to speak, and many did share their thoughts and memories. It is not possible to include those many moving statements—he was a man who was much loved and much missed. Fortunately, it is possible to include some of Nobby's own words about his early life (up until the time he left England for the United States, shortly after completion of his undergraduate studies at Oxford). He had made an autobiographical tape for his family, and with their permission it has been transcribed for inclusion here.

Jerome Neu
Santa Cruz, August 23, 2004

The cover photo was taken by his son, Thomas N. Brown. The photo on the back cover was taken on the occasion of "Awake for Finnegans Wake," a multimedia, all-night happening that Nobby organized in honor of James Joyce's great book. In the moment captured in the photograph, Nobby rises from a coffin speaking Finnegan's immortal words, "Did you think me dead?"

MEMOIRS

Norman O. Brown

This is Norman O. Brown trying to record some memoirs primarily for our children and grandchildren. It is August, 1988. On October first, will be our golden wedding. It is for me *go old and wending*. Golden wedding. Go old and wending. The pun is taken from James Joyce, *Finnegans Wake*. Trying to speak memoirs, I am reflective rather than spontaneous and in making this recording, I am going to allow myself literary and other allusions as they come into my mind. At Santa Cruz, I once gave a public autobiographical lecture trying to explain how I came to write the books that I had written. I titled the lecture "But That's Not It." I was thinking of Shakespeare's Cleopatra, trying to say goodbye to Antony: "Sir, you and I must part, but that's not it: Sir, you and I have loved, but there's not it: That you know well. Something it is I would—O, my oblivion is a very Antony, And I am all forgotten."

I have thought enough about myth and history, fact and fiction, to know that the truth cannot be told. There is always another way to tell the story. Like Hermes the Thief, I was born on a mountainside, 10,000 feet above the sea in El Oro, Mexico, above Toluca in the *Distrito Federal*, where they were mining gold. My father, Norman Charles Brown, was a very English man, but not really English. He came from Ireland, Northern Ireland, a Protestant Presbyterian Ulster man. My mother, with the beautiful, exotic name of Margarita Maria Catalina Coloma Deschwendt, was part Cuban and part German or, rather, Franco-German from Alsace. This improbable conjuncture is the beginning of a new chapter in the history of the Browns. My father was the first to break out of the circle of Anglo-Irish Protestant culture in choosing his bride. The ancient home of the Brown family was in Donaghmore, County Tyrone, Northern Ireland. I lived in Donaghmore for perhaps as long as six months. Perhaps about the age of eight; that would make it around 1921. I am not now doing any research in old letters or other records so that factual details are necessarily vague and inexact. My father brought the whole family back to Donaghmore after he left Mexico for the last time about 1921. We stayed at Aherany, the mansion or estate of cousins, the richer branch of the Brown family in Donaghmore. I remember their soap factory in the town where they made a brand of soap called Colleen to preserve that Irish girl complexion. I remember their feudal standing in the midst of the Irish peasantry, Irish and predominantly Catholic. County Tyrone was then and still is, I believe, about equally divided between Protestant and Catholic. I remember Sunday church services, for some reason not in Donaghmore but at a nearby village called something like Castlerae. I wish I still had the Bible which was given to me inscribed for ninety per cent, ninety-seven percent, answering by the Reverend McClain himself. I remember Ivybank and Balrath, mansions belonging to other members of the richer Browns. I remember Christmas carols and cousin Ada raising casuistical questions as to whether "Good King Wenceslas," which celebrates the charity of the upper classes, was really an appropriate Christmas carol for members of the upper class to sing. By this time, 1921, both my father's parents, my grandparents—whom I do not remember—were dead. I do not remember being shown any house in Donaghmore identified as the house where my father grew up. My father was the youngest of seven children: of three brothers, my uncles Willie, Sidney, and Herbert, and three sisters, my aunts Lillian, Helen, and Nita. All of these children of the humbler branch of the family emigrated from Donaghmore.

In my mind, in my imagination, my father's story begins when he was asked to take charge of his elder brother, Herbert, and emigrate with him to South Africa. My uncle Herbert was dying of TB and the high upland of the South African veldt was looked upon as the last chance to save his life. The South African veldt worked his recovery. He lived to have a large family, cousins whom I have never seen. In Bulawayo, Southern Rhodesia, he lived to commit suicide in the Great Depression of the 1930s. I remember when the news of his suicide came to us living in Bristol, my father pacing up and down in our little back garden at 102 Redland Road. My father must have been eighteen or even younger when he took his brother to South Africa. They both fought in the South African war. I have my father's medals from the South African war naming some of the great battles of the year 1900, Relief of

Ladysmith, in which he participated.

After the South African war, he got into gold mining in South Africa. Then after getting a little more technical training as a mining engineer in England, he accepted a job with the Anglo-American El Oro Mining and Railroad Company in Mexico. On the way to Mexico, he met my mother on the boat. It must have been in 1912. Who knows what really happened or what determined the outcome. I can only tell the story as a whirlwind, shipboard romance under the Caribbean moon. My mother was twenty-one-years-old or less, and ten years younger than my father. She was on her way from Germany to Havana to visit her mother's relatives for the first time. My father and my mother had at that time no common language. My father never had a foreign language more than a smattering of Spanish. My mother was a brilliant linguist, with German, Spanish and English fluent, but at that time her English must have been no better than schoolgirl English. I remember being told that my mother's Cuban relatives were very suspicious of the strange Englishman's intentions and insisted upon two weddings, one in the British consulate and another in a presumably Catholic church. The cultural divide between my father's family and my mother's family was accentuated by the World War. My mother's brother, Carlos Geier—my mother's mother married twice: Geier and Deschwendt—my uncle Carlos fought on the German side in World War I, while my father was fighting on the British side. I never met my uncle Carlos and over the years it was not the German but the Cuban side of my mother's family that played a role in my life. First my Cuban grandmother and then my uncle Pedro who lived in Havana and of whom more later.

The year of my birth, on the twenty-fifth of September, 1913, coincided with a new outbreak of violence in the Mexican Revolution, now directed against Anglo-American imperialism such as the El Oro Mining and Railroad Company. I was told that American newspapers carried my picture as the youngest refugee from Mexico. When the World War broke out, my father, who was, as I remember him even later in the thirties, a straightforward, unquestioning patriot, volunteered and served in the Royal Field Artillery. I have his medal. The great war for civilization, 1914 to 1919. While fighting in the trenches, he left his family in the Dublin area of Southern Ireland, whither his brother Willie and his sisters Nita, Lillian, and Helen had already emigrated. This was before the establishment of the Irish Free State, when Southern Ireland was still part of the United Kingdom of Great Britain and Ireland. My earliest datable memory is Armistice Day, November the eleventh, 1918. Me and my sister waving union jacks and dancing on the top of Howth Head near Dublin. Howth Castle and Environs, the scene of the action in James Joyce *Finnegans Wake*: "riverrun, past Eve and Adam's, from swerve of shore to bend of bay, brings us by a commodius vicus of recirculation back to Howth Castle and Environs."

After the war, the family returned to El Oro, Mexico. I must have been about five-years-old. We lived there till I was about eight, when we returned to England. I have a whole layer of childhood memories from this period in Mexico. They say that my sister and I were speaking Spanish to each other when we first arrived in England, and when I subsequently went back to Mexico for the first time on our honeymoon in 1938, the language did come back to me. On that trip, we had a car, and just above Toluca, we saw a road sign pointing to El Oro de Hidalgo, sixty or seventy kilometers. We did not go back. Having been born in Mexico facilitated my re-entry into the United States. Otherwise I would have had to go back to England to get a permanent Visa. I have the notion, I'm not sure how legally correct it is, that I have triple citizenship: Mexican, British, and American. I have used my Mexican identity, real or imaginary, to articulate a sense of being different from the Anglo-Saxon culture of England and, even later, America. From my childhood in El Oro, I remember fragments of the colonialist scene. The company house on which we lived, separated by a neglected tennis court from an American family living next door, the Holmeses. I remember earliest games of sexual exploration with their children. I remember the Mexican servant girl in our house, the *criada*, who was like a nurse unto us children. Her name was Maria, and I can still sing a Mexican song she taught us. [Singing]: *"Tiene los ojos tan zarcos, la norteña de mis amores; que si miro dentro de ellos, como fueron dos estrellas [in the original song, 'La norteña': me parecen los destellos], linda no llores."*

My parents' lifestyle in this period of their lives was, I think, conventionally colonialist, though not high up on the social scale. My father's position in the company was that of Chief Assayer. The house on the hillside had a magnificent view of the valley below the Mexican settlement, where the railroad ran to the junction Tultenango, and on to Mexico City. There was a company golf course. My father always liked to play golf, but couldn't afford it much later. My mother, at this stage of her life, was trying to conform. I remember her, too, dressed for golf, incompatible though this seems with her later personality. I remember parties with the bachelor contingent leading the singing: *"Little black sheep that have gone astray, and gentleman ranchers out for a spree, Lord have mercy on such as we."* That song remained a favorite of my father's, perhaps remembering his bachelor days in South Africa. I remember we had a subscription to a magazine called *Over Seas*, published by the Over Seas Club in London for Englishmen scattered throughout the world. I remember, slightly garbled, the quotation from Tennyson that appeared on the cover of every issue: "To many oceans we did sail, and founded many a mighty state. Pray God our greatness may not fail through craven fears of being great."

About 1921 (I am not stopping to verify dates), we left Mexico and returned to the Old Country. In later years, I was told that this was a sacrifice my father made in order to give his children an education, a British education. He did not belong to that upper echelon of the colonialist aristocracy which could afford to send their children back to a boarding school in England. After returning from Mexico, we stayed first in Ireland. My father, I guess, was trying to make up his mind what to do. It was at this time that we lived for some months, including Christmas, in Donaghmore as previously recorded.

The next chapter in my life story unfolds in London, two years in London, 1922, 1923; my British education began. We lived at 87 Rusthall Avenue in the West End near the Turnham Green Station on the Underground. I took the Underground everyday from Turnham Green to Earl's Court or Hammersmith to attend first a private preparatory school and then Collet Court, the official preparatory school leading to St. Paul's, one of the great English public schools. At Collet Court, my scholastic ability appeared for the first time. I remember that the whole class was ranked in individual order, and the results dictated publicly by the master. In one subject, the class list began: Cannon, Brown. And in another subject began: Brown, Cannon. This was at that time an incomprehensible joke to me. Later, but soon, I picked up the drive for competitive excellence. In Homer's phrase: "Always [??] and to excel all others."

I remember 87 Rusthall Avenue as a cramped and dingy dwelling, brightened at least part of the time by a visit of my Cuban grandmother, my mother's mother, coming from Germany, perhaps escaping from the chaotic condition of Germany at that time. Wish I could tell you more about my Cuban grandmother. I have written to her only surviving child, my uncle Pedro, still living in Miami (more about his family later), asking him if there is any record of her life. I remember her as an exuberantly vital presence, large in physique at that time, and large in manner. Instead of the conventional Spanish affectionate diminutive, *Abuelita*, little grandmother, I nicknamed her *Abuelona*. In retrospect, this period in London seems to represent the nadir of my father's fortunes. Instead of pursuing his career as a mining engineer, he seems to have ventured his savings in efforts to establish himself as a small businessman. I remember him on his bike (we never had a car), going round house to house building up an insurance practice based on weekly contributions of pennies or shillings. Also trying to make a go of our ramshackle laundry establishment; this was before the days of laundromats. And before it was over, I remember talk of emigrating again, to grow tomatoes in the Channel Islands. Or even to emigrate to Tasmania, to do what, I know not. Finally, my father got a job which lasted him throughout my childhood and until his retirement with Kepper Pass & Company, a tin mining and importing company in Bristol. We lived at 102 Redland Road, Clifton, Bristol. My father owned the house but rented out the upstairs flat. We lived on the ground floor and the basement. This was my home from 1924 to 1936. The years as a day boy at Clifton College, living at home, and the four years at Oxford, 1932 to '36 when I left for the United States.

My memory now of growing up in England is indelibly colored by the decision later to abandon England for the United States. I have grown accustomed to tell my story as of one who was not at home in England, as if I was all the time destined to break away. If you tell the story at all, it seems as if memory cannot avoid narrative conventions, such as the idea of destiny, which lend dignity or at least elementary coherence to our lives. And leaving England involved a break in the continuity of memory. There were things that had to be forgotten. Occasionally, I remember how attached I used to be to the English countryside, family holidays at the seaside in Dorset, or long bicycle trips by myself exploring Somerset or Gloucester or the mountainous region of Plynlimon in Wales. But I developed a posture of not wanting to go back and a disinclination too towards nostalgic memories. The only way I can tell this story is of one who was not at home in England. My memories of my experience at Clifton College are now structured to exhibit the drama of the outsider who makes good, a poor day boy in a boarding school and a poor scholarship boy in a very class-conscious society. A sort of second-class citizen who nevertheless obtains the pinnacle of success: head of the school and a captain of the football team. Memory has cherished moments of poignant alienation to fit this pattern. In one of our boxes of miscellaneous photographs, there is a picture of the unveiling of a statue of General Haig overlooking the Clifton College playing field. General Haig was one of the big butchers of World War I and one of Clifton College's most distinguished sons. In the picture, I, the head of the school, am standing near to Haig's daughter unveiling the statue, but the anti-imperialist tone in which

I tell this story was certainly not part of my feelings at the time. At Clifton, I absorbed the standard education of the English gentleman without questioning its validity. Absorbing a classical education without questioning its relevance. Absorbing the grim regime of intramural and intercollegiate athletics, though effective in producing hardy bodies as well as hardy English characters. In fact I may owe my lifelong good health to the regime of physical culture at Clifton. I have memories that suggest that in childhood, I had been sickly or a weakling.

I absorbed a homo-eratic…I meant, of course, to say "homoerotic," but I will leave the self-betraying slip of the tongue. I absorbed a homoerotic atmosphere of the English public school. I remember one romantic friendship. There were no girls in my life at Clifton. There were frustrative…frustrated abortive ventures into heterosexuality at Oxford. I did not really graduate into heterosexuality till I came to America.

I absorbed the conventional Church of England religiosity dispensed at Clifton Chapel, three times a week and twice on Sundays, the day boys being required to participate just like boarders. But I remember that my confirmation into the Church of

England had something fraudulent about it. It took place late in my career at Clifton as part of a deliberate effort to establish my position in the establishment, and against a background of other religious tendencies at work in my family. The seeds of dissent in me, I now think, were sown by the contradiction between the ideology I was getting at my English public school and what was going on in my family at home, with which I was in daily contact, unlike the boarders whom I so much envied. My life at home gave me access to a veritable counterculture alternative to the point of view I was being given in the English public school. This countercultural tendency I attribute entirely to my mother's influence. My mother, who I picture as having been, in our Mexican period, caught up in the conventional life of the colonialist, became in our Bristol period the driving force involving the whole family in the social consequences of her quest for an ideological framework to support her instinctive dissatisfaction with establishment orthodoxy. She had a brilliant mind, overflowing with talent. An accomplished linguist, as I remember, in English, German, French and Spanish. Also a talented musician on the violin. She had never been given higher education and the conventional training critical method and systematic self-doubt. In Bristol, her religious quest involved the family, first with the Unitarian Church and then, more extreme, with the Theosophical Society. Subsequently, her innate restlessness with any dogmatic system led her out of the Theosophical Society through anthroposophy, I think, into a secret mystical order which I think was the Order of the Golden Dawn, about which books have been written, particularly in connection with the involvement in occultism of the poet William Butler Yeats.

In my Bristol adolescence, theosophy was a real presence. Portraits of Annie Besant, Madame Blavatsky, and Krishnamurti—then being presented by Annie Besant as the new messianic master and being for a short while so accepted by my mother. The headquarters of the Theosophical Society in Bristol was the center of a countercultural social life. The turn to the East represented by theosophy poured fresh and emancipating ideas and images, such as reincarnation and karma, into the dingy life of lower-middle-class intelligentsia. I remember the aspidistras in the window. Like I said, I remember my mother as being the driving force in the family's involvement in the theosophical counterculture. My father, I believe, had lost the original Presbyterian faith so alive in my memories of Donaghmore. He was not an intellectual. I have called him a straightforward British patriot. His natural instincts were to conform. But in some incomprehensible way, he went along with my mother, at least in the outward motions. As I remember it, my reaction at the time to my mother's occultist and theosophical adventures was figureless, brattish, argumentative dissent. My life story shows that, at another level, my mother's ideas were getting under my skin, not ever to be simply discarded. But in any case, it was in this atmosphere of the home that I first learned that there were alternative cultural patterns competing for allegiance and that one had to make up one's own mind.

In my formative years in Bristol, there was life at school; there was life at home. There was also life on summer vacations—the English word is "holidays"—summer holidays in Ireland. They were not so frequent, but they bulk large in the landscape of memory, a pastoral landscape to which memory returns with relief and gladness.

Summer holidays in Ireland on the farm. Two of my father's sisters had married farmers, working farmers in what became the Irish Free State. They were Protestant gentry farmers, hard-working themselves, but employing Irish Catholic laborers on whose help they depended. They used to pay tribute to the decency of their Irish tenant laborers and of the Irish government during what they called The Time of Troubles, the emergence of the Irish Free State, 1918 to 1921. They could have been thrown out, they said, but they were not. The Protestants in the Irish Free State were well aware that they were treated better by the Catholic majority than the way the Catholic minority in Ulster was treated by the Protestant majority.

My sister Eileen and I were generously taken in for a month in the country, divided between my aunt Helen and uncle John and my aunt Lillian and uncle Harry. My aunt Helen married John Smith, whose farm was Corballis at Donabate in county Dublin. Their children, my cousins, whom I remember as playmates, were Lancelot and Stuart and Priscilla. My aunt Lillian married Harry Gill, whose farm was Ashmount Enfield Rathmolyon, county Meath. Their children were Olive and Mamie and Herbert. Corballis and Donabate had irresistible special attraction for children. There was the seaside; Corballis was on the tidal bay, looking across to

Malahide, Howth Head, and Ireland's Eye. There was the daily walk lead by my aunts Helen and Nita, through the sand dunes to the beach with the Martello Tower looking across to Lambay Island. But on both farms, there was easy-going immersion in the rhythm of farm life. Old-fashioned haying with horses. Haycocks winched up on to flat hay wagons and taken to the barn. Sheep shearing. Cattle rounded up for market. Manure being pitchforked by individual pitchfork onto the fields. There were no motorcars in the family, only ponytraps for transportation. Visiting children, my sister and I, were generously allowed to imagine they were participating in the life and work of the farm. I still have fleeting memories of the different world of the Irish Catholic laborers.

Religious services on Sunday were mandatory in both houses. The Corballis family attended somewhat perfunctorily the established Protestant Church of Ireland in Donabate. The religious life at Ashmount was more intense, more exotic, more memorable. My uncle Harry, a radiantly good-humored father-figure who included me in the circle he embraced as *evic*, Irish for "m' boy." My uncle Harry confessed that he had been a bit of a hell-raiser in his youth, hunting and all that. Perhaps even drinking, but that would be too awful to confess. My uncle Harry had been born again, and now the family at Ashmount belonged to a conventicle. Dictionary definition of "conventicle": an assembly for religious worship, especially a secret or illegal meeting for worship, in forms other than those of the established church, specifically such an assembly held by nonconformists or dissenters in England or by covenanters in Scotland. The conventicle met on Sundays in different members' houses in rotation. I remember the long ponytrap rides, and the assembly of ponytraps, which marked the place of gathering. Protestants in county Meath were scarcer than Protestants in county Dublin. This was a more vital form of religiosity for a beleaguered Protestant minority. The sect was called Cooneyites by the Protestant establishment. I have found the name of Cooney in some encyclopedia. I picked up from somewhere the knowledge that they were called "white rabbits" by the Irish peasant culture that surrounded them. I do not know what they called themselves.

I remember the religiosity of the Ashmount household, austerely puritanical without loss of good humor and generous human feelings. Profane entertainment of any kind was avoided. I believe my cousins, the younger generation, to this day have never been to a theater or movie house. I remember the conventicle meetings on Sundays. Long, long periods on my knees, waiting for another voice moved by the spirit to be raised in prayer. But I, as too young or not yet born again, was allowed to bring *Peter Rabbit* as well as a Bible to distract myself with. And I remember occasions when my older cousin, Olive, kneeling next to me, had to quiet me with tickling on my hand.

I have been back to Ireland only once since coming to the United States in 1936. I have already spoken of the necessary forgetting of the past involved in my transmigration to American soil. Beth and I made a tour of Ireland somewhere around 1978 or '80. The uncles and aunts were of course gone. We visited my cousin Lancelot at Corballis, now there installed with his wife, Stella, very much the country gentleman. That's Lancelot Smith. Also my cousin Herbert Gill at Ashmount with his wife, Nina, more like a gentleman farmer. Also my cousin Herbert's two married sisters. My cousin Olive Swanton, living in Nenagh, county Tipperary. And my cousin Mamie Bowles, living in Churchtown near Navan in county Meath. I have since heard that my cousin Herbert died relatively young and childless and the farm at Ashmount has been handed over to Olive Swanton's eldest son.

In 1932, a new phase of my life begins. 1932 to 1936 were my four years at Oxford, made possible by winning two scholarships, each worth a hundred pounds a year, which made me completely self-supporting. Although I am sure that if I had not won the scholarships, my parents would have done everything. One of the scholarships was offered by Clifton College from a special endowment to promote, to help students going from Clifton College to Balliol College, Oxford. The other was a scholarship offered by Balliol College in open competition on the basis of proficiency in the standard curriculum of classical studies. I was the top classical scholar in my year at Balliol, a position which carried some ritual obligations such as speechifying at alumni weekend, known at Oxford as Gaudy Night. Looking back on those years at Oxford, which culminated in 1936, immediately after my graduation, with my departure from England for the United States—I can't help now seeing those years at Oxford in terms of later developments and saying that the decisive thing that happened to me was the organization of my discontent with English culture into an ideology of radical political dissent. Looking back on it now, it seems to me that it happened to me rather than I did it. I was caught up in a mass movement of disaffected British intelligentsia, in my case lower-middle class. But the disaffection of my generation at Oxford with the British establishment was a mass movement. That was the significance of the scandal of the Oxford oath: *"I will not die for king and country."* When this motion was carried by a large majority in the Oxford Union, the political debating society, in which all politically interested undergraduates were voting members, the outraged Colonel Blimps among the alumni sent a sack full of white feathers, a symbol of cowardice. I picked up my white feather in remembrance of that vote. The refusal to die for king and country was not a politically serious vote in favor of pacifism, but a rejection of traditional clichés of blind obedience and mindless patriotism.

Probably the most significant political action in which I had a prominent part at Oxford was the coup by which the left captured control of the Balliol College Junior Common Room. The Junior Common Room was the apparatus of student self-government inside the College, such as it was in those days. This was a sort of revolt of the lower-middle class against the upper-class elite. The upper-class elite, represented by the most prestigious public school, the Etonians, had traditionally monopolized the presidency of the Junior Common Room. We broke up that monopoly and elected Stuart Hampshire, the philosopher, the later world-famous philosopher, as our candidate. Apart from electoral shenanigans—we put up some extra Etonian candidates to split the Etonian vote—the left campaigned on a platform to liberalize the so-called parietal rules, the rule…the rules restricting the presence of female visitors in the men's rooms. I believe my role in this not really political but cultural and very minor revolution did earn me the hostility of the establishment sector among the Balliol College dons. That must have been in 1935. The next year, 1936, which would be my last year at Oxford, we exploited the presidency of the Balliol Junior Common Room to raise money in support of the march on London of unemployed Welsh miners. On their way to London, they camped near Oxford. I remember working at the camp. Perhaps it is characteristic of my temperament that what I remember most clearly was the

Welsh miners singing, not revolutionary songs, but the Evangelical hymn: "*Bread from Heaven, bread from Heaven, feed me till I never die.*" But this local action was part of a national campaign on behalf of the unemployed, organized at that time with Communist Party participation and support.

On second thoughts, I think it is misleading to speak as I did earlier of my Oxford years as producing the organization of my discontent with English culture into an ideology of radical political dissent. It was only in America, in Chicago in 1936 to 8, that I acquired any real familiarity with the working class or with Leftism as a real political movement. Finding myself a new identity in identifying myself with the Republican cause in the Spanish Civil War and identifying myself with the mass, the great mass movement of trade union organization, which led to the formation of the CIO. It was only at the University of Wisconsin in 1939 and after, and with the help of that pioneering Marxist scholar Alban Winspear, who was my tutor there. It was only then and there that I perceived and embraced the idea of a Marxist reinterpretation of the classical tradition of high culture. At Oxford in 1932 to 6, spontaneous inchoate tendencies to the left coexisted with the body of traditional high culture being transmitted to me as my Oxford education. The traditional Oxford education was the main theme, and even if it no longer made complete sense to me, I never doubted that I had to do well at it. I took the conventional course in classical culture, Humane Letters or *Literae Humaniores*, as it was called in those days at Oxford. The program consisted of two sequences of two-year study called Mods and Greats. Mods was a program of study in Greco-Roman literature. Greats was a program of study in Greco-Roman history, Greco-Roman philosophy, and also what they called modern philosophy. At the end of each sequence, there was a public, that is to say university-wide, examination after which honors were awarded. I did indeed get first class honors in both parts, the so-called double first. In the first part, as I recall, I had no difficulty in applying myself with diligence to the study of Lucretius with Cyril Bailey, Greek lyric poetry with Bowra, Aristophanes with T.F. Higham; these are the lectures which impressed themselves most clearly on my memory. It was in the second part, and in particular in connection with modern philosophy, that the tension began to manifest itself. The tension between my own emerging point of view and the dominant trends in the culture. This is not the time to attempt an analysis of philosophy at Oxford in the 1930s.

Years later, I discovered R.G. Collingwood's autobiography in which that eccentric British philosopher indicted British philosophy as complicit in the drift of British culture towards the disaster of the Munich crisis and the loss of will to resist the rise of Fascism. Fiddling while Rome burns, lost in trivial academic disputes, insulated from European and world thought, ignorant or paying no attention to the larger questions of the interpretation of world history. But at the time I was just a very confused young man wandering in the woods of Oxford philosophy, looking for something different, something radical, something new. There was no Marx or Marxism in the Oxford curriculum or culture in those days. I think of my life-long friend, Christopher Hill, a Marxist historian, author of so many books on seventeenth-century England and the English Revolution, and became Master of Balliol in the 1960s, as having spent his life stuffing Marxism down the throats of the British and specifically Oxford establishment. At Oxford in the

1930s, the new thing was the new philosophy of language derived from Wittgenstein which became, and has been, the dominant trend in Anglo-speaking philosophy on both sides of the Atlantic during my lifetime. Very much later in my life, after exposure to Freud and psychoanalytical ideas, I was able to see the possible role of a new philosophy of language in the making of a cultural revolution. French structuralist philosophy in my lifetime has some achievements to its credit along these lines, most prominently associated with the name of Lacan, attempting a synthesis of Freud and Marx on the basis of a new philosophy of language. In my work, in *Life Against Death*, the chapter on "Language and Eros" is quite immature. It is only in *Love's Body* and with the turn to poetry as well as psychoanalysis, or the turn to a poetic interpretation of psychoanalysis, that a new approach to language really enters the picture. The Oxford philosophy of language, based on a marriage of Wittgenstein and traditional British empiricism, and innocent of any Freudian admixture, had no such revolutionary or emancipatory potential. It never really got to be more than an expression of conventional academic skepticism and British parochial insulation from

European thought, a convenient ideology for academic intelligentsia voting for the Liberal or the Labour Party in the period after World War II. Stuart Hampshire's life-long project to fortify this bland potion by an admixture of psychoanalytical radicalism was never carried through.

In my final examination at Oxford, I did not think that I understood what was going on in philosophy and concentrated my effort to excel in ancient history. But it turned out that my first class honors were achieved in philosophy. I spent the whole three hours of the examination writing an answer to one question: "do propositions exist?" I believe the grand conclusion I reached was that they do not exist but they subsist. I am grateful that my later Marxist reorientation has left me with no sympathy for such parlor games of academic philosophizing.

The only one of my teachers at Oxford whose memory I cherish and whom I remained in touch with, is Isaiah Berlin who was then a fellow of All Souls College. It was lucky for me that I was farmed out from Balliol to be tutored in philosophy by him. He was then doing philosophy in the then-fashionable way. My copy of Ayer's book on *Language, Truth and Logic* was bought by me when I was still at Balliol in 1936, but Berlin was always doing much more than that, in touch with European thought in a way that made him unique not only in Oxford but in England as a whole. Isaiah Berlin was then writing his book on Karl Marx, an anti-Marxist book on Karl Marx. I think he helped introduce me to the complexities of interpreting the early humanistic writings of Karl Marx, then being published for the first time. I think he also encouraged me to apply for a Commonwealth Fund fellowship to study at a university in the United States of America.

Undergraduate friends at Oxford. I have mentioned the names of the only two that I have kept up with: Stuart Hampshire and Christopher Hill. Keeping up with Stuart Hampshire was made easier by his immigration to the United States. I do not think that our friendship ever amounted to deep reciprocal influence although I did greatly admire his book on Spinoza, finding in Spinoza a model for a radical, progressive, materialist point of view. And already in 1951 drawing attention to the connection between Spinoza and Freud. It was otherwise with Christopher Hill. He was congenial to me from the start as a lower-middle class outsider or intruder into the Oxford establishment. I remember the nonconformist religious atmosphere in his parents' home in York whence we set out together to walk on the Yorkshire moors. By coincidence of fate or fortune, he was not only an intellectual but, like me, also a rugby football athlete. We were on the same team when Balliol won the intercollegiate cup at Oxford; it must have been the year 1934. So he was the only one who shared with me membership in three distinct social worlds at Oxford: the rugger heavies, the political radicals, and the intellectual aesthetic elite. The most important moment in our association and, in memory retrospect, one of the high spots of my life, was the trip Christopher and I took together to Germany to learn the language in the summer of 1934 just after Hitler came to power. Going to Freiburg in Breisgau, where we stayed in the home of Herr Polizei Major Aufhammer, the police chief, an old social democrat trying to keep his job under the new regime and trying to keep his family together when his two sons, along with the vast majority of German youth, had lost their heads and hearts to Adolf Hitler. Christopher and I spent beautiful days walking in the Black Forest. I can no longer remember any specific topics of our endless conversations, but I cannot doubt that we reinforced in each other the attraction to Marxism. It would take a big book to compare and contrast my relation to Marxism with Christopher Hill's. Seen from the outside, we might seem to have gone different ways. I began to explore for a passage to a post-Marxist world after the defeat, in 1948 in the presidential election in the United States of America, in which I saw my expectation for a mass movement of the left behind the candidacy of Henry Wallace refuted. So I moved on to a psychoanalytic perspective in *Life Against Death* and even more visionary or meta-rational perspectives in *Love's Body*. Christopher Hill stayed with a Marxist framework and spent his life introducing flexibility, subtlety, sophistication into a Marxist interpretation of the seventeenth-century English Revolution. But as Heraclitus said, "The unseen harmony is stronger than the seen." From his vast array of writings, I pick out two for their hidden connection with major themes in my work. His 1955 essay on "Clarissa Harlow and Her Times" is a brilliant exposition of the connection between economic and sexual exploitation in the modern, bourgeois, patriarchal family. His masterpiece on radical, utopian, communal religiosity and the English Revolution, *The World Turned Upside Down*, 1972, has an uncanny relation to the intoxicated, Dionysian tendencies erupting in *Love's Body* and in the worldwide cultural upheaval of the 1960s.

This concludes what I want to attempt in this first installment of memoirs taking the story down to my departure for the United States in 1936.

IN MEMORIAM
NORMAN O. BROWN

Sept. 25, 1913–Oct. 2, 2002

A Ceremony at
the University of California, Santa Cruz
October 19, 2002

Jerome Neu

We are gathered to celebrate the life of Norman O. (Nobby) Brown.

Nobby himself was uneasy about funerals and celebrations of the dead. In *Closing Time*, he quoted a passage about Vico's farce of a funeral. The faculty of the University of Naples fought (literally fought) over the honor of carrying Vico's bier. "As no amicable understanding could be reached, the Confraternity, with small regard for human decency, decided to take their leave, abandoning the corpse where it lay" [p.12]. But Nobby, in his dialectical way, juxtaposed the passage about Vico's funeral with words from Joyce's *Finnegans Wake*: "Lovesoftfun at Finnegan's Wake" [p.13, FW 607].

Nobby changed lives with his books. He changed lives with his person. He was a liberating, visionary scholar, the successor in the twentieth century to

Blake and to Nietzsche. He was a model of what a teacher, a colleague, and an engaged intellectual should be. A true friend, he would walk and talk with us friends, genuinely interested in what we were thinking, and interested in provoking us to think better and to be better. He himself was the best of us. I miss the twinkle in his eye and the mischief and merriment in his manner. I miss Nobby.

He himself was always changing, always discovering and rediscovering. He lived by the biblical epigraph he chose for his last book, *Apocalypse and/or Metamorphosis*: "And be not conformed to this world [*be nonconformists*]; but be ye transformed [*metamorphose yourselves*] by the renewing of your mind" (*Romans* 12:2). While Nobby was always on the edge with his thought, his wife Beth (who is here with us today) kept him stable in his daily life, and we, as much as Nobby and for Nobby, owe her an immense debt of gratitude. Because Nobby was always developing, I fear that whatever I might say about the content of his thought would be partial and incomplete, and so we would have to conclude, as Nobby himself once did, speaking of each of the stages of his own development, "but that's not it." So I will continue to speak here more of the manner than the matter of his thought.

While Nobby was a mesmerizing sort of guru, he didn't much care for slavish disciples. He wanted us to be ourselves, only better. He wanted us to think for ourselves. I dedicated a book to him once, writing: "to Norman O. Brown, who argued with me every inch of the way." He argued with us all every inch of the way. He scowled at us, he mocked us, he charmed, and flirted, and provoked. Like Freud, he was not optimistic about the human condition, but he sought to understand it, and to make it better, and he was a true democrat in his love for the individuals who must suffer together through its travails. He was moved by the Dionysian spirit, seeking always to "make it new" and to make it fun. He organized a riotous wake for *Finnegans Wake* at UCSC. But he was also a Roman soldier of a citizen, devoted to the dutiful improvement of the University—going to the meetings and doing the behind-the-scenes work that keeps things going. He was equally engaged with the wider world of politics, with our shared public life. Everyone's life. (Joyce's HCE, "Here Comes Everybody.") Most of all, like Socrates, he was a masterful teacher, and again like Socrates, he was not conventionally "nice." Nobby was unsettling.

Sometimes he pronounced, but most often (in one-on-one encounters) he questioned and he probed, making many feel less comfortable and less secure, but all the same generously bringing and getting the best out of those he engaged. He also learned from others. He sought to understand the world from radically different philosophical, political, and religious perspectives. He didn't simply read, absorb, and critique—as professors do—those he referred to as "my authorities, my authors," that is, the "great company" that appeared in his many quotations [*Love's Body* Acknowledgements]. He *inhabited* (truly inhabited) different systems of thought from Marxism to Freudianism, from Maoism to Islam. He constantly changed, constantly developed, constantly renewed his mind. I remember the occasion when he announced to his old friend Herbert Marcuse that this year he was a Jew. (Marcuse responded with, "I won't come to the bar mitzvah, but I will come to the bris.") In Nobby's last years of thinking, like his friend John Cage, he was gripped by chance. But it was not by chance that his attachments to individuals and his commitment to love and to unity (the notion that "we are all members of one body") never faltered.

While Nobby was deeply serious, he was also playful and the *NY Times* obituary writer rightly described him as "an erudite and spectacularly playful philosopher." Nobby was about 60 when I met him thirty years ago. I never thought about his age, but if I had, for the better part of those after-sixty years I would have said he was about 40. It is an encouraging thought. It means it is possible to remain young in spirit, vibrantly alive, overflowing with the energy to invigorate and enrich others during what are often thought of as the sunset years. As one of Nobby's poets, William Blake, said: "Energy is the only life and is from the body…Energy is eternal delight." For all his learning and weighty thoughts, Nobby was energetically playful almost to the end—when Alzheimer's took its toll. The example of Nobby's life gives me hope, a model of how to live as I (and perhaps some of you) head towards the sunset.

Let me conclude with another bit of poetry. Nobby had taped to his study door the following lines from Shelley's "Ode to the West Wind," written out in Nobby's own hand and headed: "Here is my Shelley:"

Be thou, Spirit fierce,
My spirit! Be thou me, impetuous one!

Drive my dead thoughts over the universe
Like withered leaves to quicken a new birth;
And, by the incantation of this verse,

Scatter, as from an unextinguished hearth
Ashes and sparks, my words among mankind!
Be through my lips to unawakened earth

The trumpet of a prophecy!

James Clifford

Each of us knew a particular Nobby. This is mine…

I knew him as a younger colleague. When I interviewed for a job in HistCon, he took me for a walk in what seemed then like an endless labyrinth of fire trails above the campus. By the end I was completely wrung out from his relentless questions—exhausted, yet somehow exhilarated.

Nobby gave something very important to a young scholar: he took you seriously. There wasn't much small talk on those walks. You had to come up with something that was "news." It was as if you were always reporting from the front lines. And so you struggled to meet the challenge, and sometimes you even convinced yourself that you had.

The conversations were ongoing. He stayed in touch. Every now and then I would get short, sometimes gnomic, letters from him. Perhaps a response to a book review I had written, or a reference connected to some previous exchange. The notes turned up in my Kresge mailbox: small, sealed manila envelopes, neatly addressed. No multi-use envelopes for these communiqués! No post-its with "f.y.i."

Recently I came across one of them, stuck in a book of Charles Olson's poems. Let me share it with you...

> Jim
> I am intoxicated by this little quote—M. Moore on H. James—on what it is to be American; I want to share it with somebody. I thought it might appeal to your sense of geography, and action (=Olson on Melville etc.
> NOB

And taped to the sheet the passage from Marianne Moore:

> Some complain of his [Henry James's] transferred citizenship as a loss; but when we consider the trend of his fiction and his uncompromising denouements, we have no scruple about insisting that he was American; not if the American is, as he thought "intrinsically and actively ample...reaching westward, southward, any-

where, everywhere," with a mind "incapable of the shut door in any direction."

Nobby had many alter-egos. Henry James, here, is an American who chose English citizenship, the opposite of Brown, who left England for America. Nobby's projects and life choices always had to be, at some level, world historical. What was this "America" he had given himself to? We talked about that: about my hero, William Carlos Williams, Nobby's entanglement with the more troubling Ezra Pound, and Charles Olson representing, perhaps, a kind of synthesis. In any event, a way forward in that American poetic tradition, leading on to contemporary poets we both admired like Susan Howe…

Nobby knew a lot of poetry by heart. I'll never forget walking into the Kresge Steno pool to find him reciting the whole of Keats "Ode to Psyche" for Betsy Wooten and her colleagues. ("…A bright torch, and a casement ope at night/To let the warm Love in!" Some steno pool!) I later asked Nobby to recite it at my wedding.

I don't have much poetry memorized. But on that very first walk, we talked about some lines from

"Maximus to Himself" that I had managed to remember:

Olson:
>It is undone business
>I speak of, this morning
>with the sea
>Stretching out
>From my feet

America was undone business for Nobby; and it was big, fundamentally expansive…

I worried about that: Olson's Melville at the whale ship's masthead, striding like a giant across the Pacific Ocean, Henry James's active ampleness… "reaching westward, southward, anywhere, everywhere…" Weren't these just evocations of imperial ambition?

We argued about this. Thinking big wasn't a problem for Nobby. He was a revolutionary thinker who wanted to be in tune with a really expansive history that would make everything (as Joyce put it in *Finnegans Wake*) "roll wholly over." And he didn't shrink from visions of violent change. (What would he say about today's universal adversary, "the terrorist"?)

When I took refuge, as I often did, in appeals to diversity and cultural relativism, he would say: "Well, we Marxists..." or "We Muslims..."

Yet if there was an undeniable universalism in Nobby's prophetic tradition, made up of braided Greek, Hebrew, Christian, Islamic, and American elements, this was not in any ordinary sense a closed or ethnocentric vision. For Nobby's universalism was always undone business. It was always looking for ways to be retranslated, made new. And the heretic, the prophet, and yes, the terrorist, were always in the wings, ready to unmake any finality or earthly dominion.

And there was the amazing example—which many of us were roped into—of his late, serious, engagement with Islam. It went on, at high intensity, for several years. Interlibrary loan worked overtime! I recall, more than once, meeting Nobby leaving the library on Friday afternoon, clasping a big pile of books for weekend processing.

And even though, as with all his detours and alter-egos, the path to Islam eventually led back to Blake, to *Finnegans Wake* and the rest, the sustained effort to understand was remarkable and deep.

How little this restless, expansive interest has in

common with today's arrogant, ignorant imperialism! How unlike the repressive moralism that now rules our land, slamming shut the open doors of Norman O. Brown's America!

I really miss having Nobby around, to talk about these things.

Christopher Connery

Norman O. Brown—Revolutionary.

No doubt my title will give some of you the shock of misrecognition that I've felt listening to other versions of Nobby's life today.

Norman O. Brown, Revolutionary? But that's not it.

Well, so be it.

I studied with Nobby as an undergraduate, and like many of his friends here, had my mind blown on walks in the woods—the best part of my life at UCSC—after I came back here to teach. I still teach Nobby's work, in a course called The 1960s. The course is about world revolution. I teach his work alongside Mao, Guevara, Fanon, Debord, the Weather Underground. He came to my class in the spring of 1992, and he was happy to have his work considered in that company. In that class, he met undergraduate

...ca Herzig, who's flown out for this event from Bates College in Maine, where she teaches. She was one of the latest—maybe the very latest—in that long line of us who walked and talked with Nobby.

Nobby's was first and last a revolutionary project. Transformation, metamorphosis, ending, apocalypse: these were to be historical phenomena, never merely psychic, but in the world. In the demonstrations after the bombing in Cambodia, he was there, intoning with glee, "western civilization is over." It was one of his deepest hopes.

He gave instructions to protest marchers. In the *Book of Ours*, the course pamphlet he wrote with Nor Hall:

"Political protests should be processions
'it's a good day for an epiphany.'"

Protest marches should be processions—dionysian processions, with poetry, dancing, gods. But it really was about revolution: about ending this thing we're in. More of Berkeley than of Beijing, and never quite the party line, the program of the Communist Party. But Brown belongs with the revolutionaries. When I teach him in my 1960s course, he is not a soft and spiritual foil to Che, Fanon, and Mao. He shares their project, and my students immediately understand this.

"Peace and love" was not his slogan. He often told a story about writing Chapter Ten of *Love's Body*. He had gone to an anti-nuclear rally, listened to the speeches, to the tonality of the crowd, and had seen that this was not his way. He went home and wrote the chapter FIRE.

> To bring this world to an end, in a final conflagration, or explosion, bursting the boundaries.
>
> The final conflagration, or apocalypse. The unity of life and death as fire.
>
> A fiery consummation. Not suspense, but end-pleasure, not partial sacrifice (castration) but total holocaust.
>
> Not peace but a sword. Peace lies in finding the true war. The reconciliation of opposites, the making of friendship, takes place on the battlefield.
>
> The thing, then, is not to abolish war, but to find the true war. Open the hidden Heart in Wars of Mutual Benevolence, Wars of Love.

His turn to Islam was the search for the true war. There will be no more secular revolutions. The true war would need poetry, yes, and it would need prophets. Prophets who would not only give instructions for protest marches, remind us of revolutions' returnings and revolvings, but who would show us who the real revolutionaries were.

Nobby never became a "post-Marxist," but he left behind Marxist science and Marxist rationality. He never left behind the belief in and hope for the break, the strategic moment, the leap into the unknown, that Lenin and Mao found in revolution itself. A prophet of the mass line. Nobby: Maoist.

In his last public lecture at UCSC, inspired by the uprising in East Berlin that brought down the wall, he found revolutionary energy within consumption itself, within the impossibility of its fiery desire. In Kresge Town Hall, Nobby quoting Mick Jagger—"I can't get no. Satisfaction." Nobby understood what Trotsky and Mao called permanent revolution.

He never talked of the 1960s as failed. And now more than ever, it's important to resist the tide of reaction that wants to bury the 1960s, or deny its revolutionary character, or see it as the perversion of noble left traditions. We must resist the discourse of failure itself. But Nobby did talk often about one of the 60s failings, and he said over and over, when we spoke of the 60s in the Pogonip, or in Wilder Ranch, that as a movement it had failed to come to terms with death. It was a concern he shared with Robert Jay Lifton, and we talked about Lifton's study of the Chinese Cultural Revolution, *Revolutionary Immortality*—the animating force of the Cultural Revolution being the fear of the death of the Chinese revolution.

That coming to terms with death was, I think, at the heart of the work with *Finnegans Wake*, and its hero of the mass line, HCE—Here Comes Everybody. It was at the heart of the turn, late in his intellectual life, to biology, to the species, to, in one of his favorite passages from Marx, from the *Economic and Philosophical Manuscripts of 1844*, the *Gattungswesen*, the species being:

"Death appears as the harsh victory of the species over the particular individual and seems to contradict their unity; but the particular individual is only a determinate species being, and thus mortal."

Only a determinate species being. I will teach Nobby again this spring. I will mourn him and miss him. For much of what I have learned about hope, revolutionary hope, I learned from him. I'll do what I can to keep it alive.

Nathaniel Mackey

When Jerry invited me to speak at this celebration of Nobby's life he quoted Nobby's statement at the end of *Love's Body* that "there is only poetry," recalling the importance of poetry and poets to Nobby's work and thought. He anticipated a point I'd wish to make. In addition to being a dear personal friend whom I will miss and already miss and have in fact missed for a few years now due to the decline in his health, Nobby was a great friend of poetry, one of those who'd qualify for the great audience Whitman said there has to be for there to be great poetry. It was Nobby who invited the San Francisco/Black Mountain poet Robert Duncan to teach here at UCSC in the 1960s and it was a shared attachment to the work of the Black Mountain poets (Charles Olson, Denise Levertov, Robert Creeley and Edward Dorn in addition to Duncan) and their modernist predecessors William Carlos Williams, H.D. and

Ezra Pound that sparked our friendship when I began teaching here in 1979.

Nine years ago Nobby gave me, for my birthday, his complete set of the little magazine *Caterpillar*, an experimental poetry journal edited by Clayton Eshleman that ran from 1967 to 1973. A few years earlier he had promised to leave it to me upon his death (Nobby not infrequently spoke of aging and death and dying and his own approaching death), so there was a sad, elegiac feeling to my receipt of it if not to his giving it. It seemed he was beginning to say goodbye. But the gift returned me to the beginning of my engagement with Nobby's work, as one of the first things of his I'd read was the Frederick William Atherton lecture he gave at Harvard in 1967, a lecture called "From Politics to Metapolitics" which appeared in the first issue of *Caterpillar* and in which the aphoristic mode and the verse-like ventilation he resorted to in *Love's Body* began to be taken farther. There we find such propositions as:

Beyond the reality-principle is poetry
                       taking metaphors seriously
                       (metaphors and analogies)
                       that way madness lies.

And:

> The language of healing, or making whole, is not psychoanalysis, but poetry.
> Poetry   is the visionary form, or explosion
>   which overthrows the reality-principle
>   and transforms the world, just the way it is,
>   without changing a thing
>   the transformation is the unification.

Nobby's friendship with poetry was not an easy one. His was a very tall order to fill. He continued to have great expectations and to make strong demands on poetry in a period in which most people, most poets included, no longer do. I recall him voicing a lukewarm reaction to John Ashbery's work, complaining that there wasn't enough religion in it. What Nobby wanted and valued most was a vatic poetry, a prophetic poetry, a poetry of apocalyptic announcement. I remember walking up the steps with him to our offices at Kresge one morning in the early eighties as he cited Olson's quotation, in full, of "The Sea Marke," an otherwise unremarkable poem by the seventeenth-century explorer John Smith, in *The Maximus Poems*. "He's saying," Nobby insisted, "there's been a shipwreck, we're sunk."

To his credit, however, Nobby was hesitant and of more than one mind when it came to vatic vocation. The first time I heard him speak was in the early seventies—it was 1971 I think—at Stanford. The talk, which was in the collagelike, mythographic vein of "Daphne, or Metamorphosis" and "Metamorphoses II: Actaeon" and was in fact, if my memory can be trusted, an early draft of the latter, was called "To Greet the Return of the Gods" or, if I've misremembered the title, at least made use of that line from H.D.'s *Tribute to Freud*. What I most clearly remember is that rather than reading the piece to us that evening Nobby played a tape recording of himself reading the piece. He explained that the piece called for a priestly voice, a voice he wasn't sure he could call up at will or summon before an audience. He'd taken the precaution, he explained, of recording it beforehand. He then turned the tape recorder on and sat down, facing it, in the front row, nervously pouring himself repeated cups of wine throughout the talk. It was odd, a bit like a Samuel Beckett play. After the tape concluded and after the applause Nobby invited criticisms of the piece and when, after a couple of minutes, none came forth, he said, "Okay, I'll go first," and began by saying, "Well, for one thing, it's too masochistic." Likewise, when he asked me about the limits of Duncan's influence on my work one day and I answered by quoting two lines from Duncan's "Transgressing the Real," "my thoughts are servants of the stars, and my words /...come from a mouth that is the Universe," lines the likes of which I swore I'd never be caught writing, he laughed approvingly—and with a touch of that schoolboy mischief he had a way of calling to mind.

I've been thinking a lot about Nobby's laughter these last two weeks, a lot about conversations with Nobby, a lot about Nobby's friendship not only with poetry but with so many people, myself luckily among them. His eminence and celebrity notwithstanding, he managed to be not only a friend but, even better, a buddy, capable even of a form of that thing buddies take together, the road trip. Who but Nobby could one drive to New College in San Francisco with to hear Susan Howe speak on Emily Dickinson, drive to San Jose State with for an H.D. conference, drive to Berkeley with for a meeting of the International Ibn al-Arabi Society? Nobby gave new meaning to the word "colleague," sharing his interests and his work and engaging one's own with unique generosity and severity both, provocative and catalytic. Then, too, there were those walks he took so many of us on, those floating seminars he conducted thru the woods and along the beach. One of them in particular keeps coming back to me these last two weeks, a walk he and I took on the beach one sunny winter afternoon during the mid-eighties, Nobby talking, among many things, about H.D. and Pound, the prophetic tradition, the aging of his friends and his own aging, the sun reflected on the water a ribbon or a rug or a bridge of white light...

"There is only poetry"—meager, we find at moments like this, modest and valedictory, beginning again and again to say goodbye. And so, even so, to end, a poem:

> Never not another bridge to
> cross, not before then so
>   stark. We were beginning to be
>   dead it seemed. Sought
>   silence's
>   counsel, wise in that way,
>   leaning toward light,
>   off-balance... Had it been a
>   boat we'd have gone under,
>   a
> car we'd have slid into a ditch...

It wasn't riskless we imagined
we'd be but not defenseless. A
　feather broke our fall. We breathed
in... Light met the moment we left
　　　　　　　　　　　　left us
　　breathless, lidless, looking up at
　the sun. It wasn't ecstasy as yet
　　　but we kept hoping. A feast
　　　had been set we'd been told...
A token rope let down from the
　　　　　　　　　　　　　sky
　　hung out of reach and began to
　　　　　　　　　　　　　unravel,
wind what we took to be rope...

　On Lone Coast we'd seen a runway
of sparks, light bouncing off
　　water, the sun itself drawn
　out, reflected on water... A
　　　　　　　　　　　　carpet
　　of sparks inviting flight...
　Rung wound in with rug, lit
　　runner... Auspice we took it
　　　　　　　　　　　　to be...
The bridge we began with vanished.
If not a runway and a rug it wasn't
　there. No way could we have walked
　it. We wanted it even so. A bed

                              of hot
           coals it would've been, carpet of
                                     scars...
        Bridge being what it was, we turned
            away. The two whose remnants we
          were stood at our backs, we
              their whispered regret...
                                  A
     rug of white light on the bay, late
    sun. "If by the end there's been a
    sign this will have been it." So we
        thought or said we thought, though
                                    by the
         end there'd be no sign. It wasn't signs
         we were after, we sought what signs
            replaced, pitiless wish to be all
          there, that it all be there... It
                                was a
   healing song we sang had there been a song
                                               we
      sang, a soothing song, Wagogo we'd have
    been. A winding sound we'd have made
         had there been a sound we made. Zeze
                                       bowed
       by raffia, mbira plucked by thumbs,
           a grinding sound we made had we
          made a sound... But by the end there'd
             be no sound, sign's mute witness

    rescinded as well, white rug's amalgam
                               of water
  and sun now neither water nor sun… It
    was a dream drummed into the air we
  took in, a brink we backed away from,
                                 rickety
  bridge. Had there been a song we sang it was
  extremity we sang, all but strangling song,
                                       a

straining
song

Robert Meister

I have thought about this day since Nobby began his long decline, and still I am not ready. Today is too soon for me to place my dear, dear friend in the common history of our lifetime; it is already too late to thank him for his singular place in my own life's encounter with this history. And so, I want to talk today, not about NOB the great man whose achievement will be measured in the work of fellow luminaries, but about Nobby the intellectual companion whom I thought *with* and thought *about* on my best days in Santa Cruz over twenty-five years; about Nobby the friend with whom I shared my closest friends, as he shared his; and about Nobby the family man with whom I shared my family—Ritu, Andrew, and Tom, who also mourn his loss.

I still visualize that Nobby ceremoniously carving Beth's Thanksgiving turkey; at my sons'

Saturday morning soccer games, where we sat in the bleachers, each reading aloud the other's writing on disgust and putrefaction in the work of Bataille; on long walks in Fall Creek and Nisene Marks with little Andrew on my shoulders, drumming on my head "Daddy, Nobby, discuss-discuss, Plato Aristotle, Hegel, Marx"—and clapping when we stopped and squared off face-to-face, as Nobby liked to do. If my sons ever understand who I was and wanted to be in the years of their childhood, I like to think it is from remembering, now, how his presence brought me to life.

And when they grow older, I hope that they may come to understand how he also brought me to death—and this in many senses. "There isn't enough death in you—or in Marx," Nobby said, after I finally published the Marx book that he and I had discussed in every version over a fifteen-year period. Dwelling on death, I said, is not a way to "stay alive in history"—a phrase he had only recently coined, but that accurately described his many handwritten notes to me on his daily reading of the foreign and domestic press. During my years as a recipient of those notes, when our discussions focused on world politics and the long collapse of communism, I had not reread *Life Against Death* or *Love's Body*. (I had read them as an undergraduate—long before I knew the man himself.) But now, Nobby brought me up short: "Suppose," he said, "that the East Germans had produced a genuinely good Trabant—a true *Volkswagen* that eliminated the need for planned obsolescence. Would Marxism then have had a chance?"

His point, of course, was that "Actually Existing Communism" (a phrase he took from Rudolf Bahro) had failed because it was just another Puritanism, and that Bahro's Green alternative (with which Nobby also flirted) was doomed for the same reason —it was simply "eco-Calvinism," as we came to call it on our walks. At another level, however, his question to me was also a rare moment of convergence between my daily companion, Nobby, and the world's Norman O. Brown—it was a critique of "Plato-Aristotle-Hegel-Marx" from the standpoint of a Dionysian Christian—it was an anti-Calvinist reading of St. Paul.

Nobby's point, as always, was also political: that the fall of communism did not reveal the superiority of capitalist ideas, but rather a misconception of human desire shared by both communism and capitalism—the misconception that desire is the pursuit of happiness. Against this view, Nobby revised ("revisioned," he would say), the last fifty years of his own thought as the Freudian unconscious of the Cold War itself. He concluded that we do not spend in order to get, but rather get in order to spend—that our apparent desire for gain is not self-explanatory; it is rather a response to a socially-grounded fear of our deeper desire for loss; that, if fear of loss is the source of human bondage, then losing itself—the enjoyment of loss—may be the closest we humans ever get to freedom. Nobby, at the end of his long love affair with Americanism, came to see that human happiness is not the goal—it is not even *a* goal—of human struggle and pursuit. Just yesterday, I read a phrase in Slavoj Žižek that brought thoughts of Nobby flooding back: "In psychoanalysis the betrayal of desire has a precise name: happiness." (*Welcome to the Desert of the Real*, p. 58)

The idea that happiness betrays desire is a key, I think, to Nobby's identification in his last years with what his friend Christopher Hill called "the experience of defeat." By the end (we can now speak of an end), Nobby did not see the experience of defeat as a symptom of failed prophecy. He saw it, rather, as the essence of "the prophetic tradition"—the lineage of beautiful losers which we come to celebrate today, and to mourn, on the occasion of Nobby's loss.

It is natural in eulogizing great thinkers to mine their own words for epitaphs: the problem here is that Nobby did nothing but write his own epitaph, clearly hoping to frustrate the likes of us on just this occasion. Given the plethora of contradictory quotes from him that sum up his work, the best way to honor Nobby's mind, I am tempted to say, would be for me to disagree with all of the other eulogies that will be offered today. But this would be to dishonor the body, the *corpus* as he might call it, and Nobby was a model of decorum when it came to honoring bodies.

And so, I will not fight over Nobby's body with those of you who share my grief over his loss and my guilt over the past few years. Instead, I will take issue with the figure of Norman O. Brown, himself—fondly and insistently, as I would if my friend Nobby were in the room. In the face of the brute facts, and against everything Nobby wrote, I want to deny his death in just the way that he did for the 29 years in which we were friends and companions.

I want to do this by reflecting on *why* we were

friends and companions—why *me*, why each of us—when Nobby could have defined himself through his relationship to the great luminaries (Marcuse, Cage, Schorske, Jameson, and so forth) with whom he brought me to dinner or on walks. The answer, I think, lies in his passionate wish to "stay alive" (as he later said), by shedding his own intellectual skin and becoming someone new.

If I had not known Nobby, my idea of intellectual integrity would have centered on ideas of consistency and self-defense—sticking to my guns with ever-stronger arguments for the views that I had previously expressed. I would have made a career of sorts, condemning the opportunism of the gurus on the left and right who flatter their audience by seeking agreement. Nobby's friendship showed me a better form of intellectual integrity—an openness to renewal accompanied by an absolute refusal to flatter anyone, least of all one's friends. Were it not for Nobby, I would not have known that intellectual integrity must include the project of "staying alive."

And, so it would be unbecoming for me to close by saying how flattered I was by Nobby's friendship, which began when he was so distinguished, and I so young (like the others who have spoken thus far). A better conclusion is that, as I grow old, my intellectual friends must always include the young—that this is my own best hope of working with integrity, of "staying alive."

On the night of Nobby's death, I went and said good-bye to his body. I told him how sorry I was that I had not been able to accept the loss of his mind, and to be the companion he needed in his final years. This is, no doubt, a failing of mine, about which Nobby's writings have much to teach. But Nobby, my dear friend, I will never say good-bye to your mind.

Helene Moglen

Three or four days after Nobby's death, a few of us—who had frequently "walked with Nobby"— had, what we called, a "wake"—for him.
We called it "a wake" because we thought it was something to which he would not, in any event, have objected—
And that it might even be something of which he would have mildly approved.

It had been a very warm day—and, as dusk turned to night, we sat on my deck, overlooking the city and bay, talking quietly.
Suddenly—there was—a-disturbance-in the air— almost a shock—
and the lights went out.
My house was dark—as were a small line of houses around my house—but the rest of the street—

The rest of the city—remained illuminated.

We sat then for about an hour in candlelight—outside on this warm Sunday evening—talking about Nobby—
Remembering.

When suddenly—the fireworks began:
And the sky was filled with wonderful explosions of color:
colors erupting within colors; the transmutation of one color into another—and then another:
intensities of light—increasing, deepening, fading, falling.

In one sense, there was no mystery of course:
we had simply forgotten.
It was the first Sunday in October—when Santa Cruz celebrates the departure of tourists and the return of Autumn.

There was no mystery—
and yet
in the days since—my mind has returned to the uncanny juxtaposition of those events.

The unexpected, unaccountable fall into darkness
The unanticipated explosion of light.

It seemed that Nobby was a man of just such contrasts and contradictions:
    a personality remote and intensely present,
    a mystic and a scholar,
    an intellectual renegade who respected structures (if not figures) of authority,

Perhaps, most of all, Nobby was a man capable of apocalyptic and utopian imaginings.
Dark and light visions,
which are nowhere more evident,
nowhere more distilled—
Than they are in his extraordinary Phi Beta Kappa Address of May 1960: an intellectually bold manifesto: "APOCALYPSE: The Place of Mystery in the Life of the Mind"

Writing at a moment that seems in so many ways to prefigure the present moment, he muses:

> And so there comes a time—I believe we are in such a time—when civilization has to be renewed by the

discovery of new mysteries, by the undemocratic but sovereign power of the imagination, by the undemocratic power which makes poets the unacknowledged legislators of mankind, the power which makes all things new.

Delivering this subversive speech at a distinguished university to a group of gifted and aspiring scholars, Nobby insisted that social, political and intellectual renewal were possible only through the transformative power of the deeply personal, libidinally invested, prophetic imagination.

He feared—above all—the hardening of thought, the paralysis of dogma, the fetishization of the book. Looking back to Emerson's Phi Beta Kappa address, "The American Scholar," he welcomed—and quoted—what he described as Emerson's "Transcendentalist anticipation of what I want to say:"

> The sacredness which attaches to the act of creation, is transferred to the record. Instantly the book becomes noxious: the guide is a tyrant. The sluggish and perverted mind of the multitude, having once received this book, stands upon it and makes an outcry if it is destroyed. Colleges are built upon it. Meek young men

> grow up in libraries. Here, instead of Man Thinking we have the bookworm. I had better never see a book than to be warped by its attraction clean out of my own orbit, and make a satellite instead of a system. The one thing in the world of value is the active soul.

It was the active soul, the creative soul—in this sense, the playful soul, that was at the heart of Nobby's project as a teacher, a scholar, a colleague, and even—a friend.

It was his desire to model the active soul that drove Nobby as a teacher:
a teacher of undergraduates to whom, he once told me, he wanted to be of use; a teacher of faculty and graduate student colleagues—for whom he taught a memorable seminar, with Carl Schorske, on Goethe's *Faust* and to whom he presented an extraordinary series of lectures on Islam.

It was his desire to invigorate and articulate that active soul—the informed and ecstatic imagination—that motivated his intensely experienced, poetic prose, which was also always a form of visionary reading: the ecstatic yet respectful making of the other into the self.

It was the desire "to see with his own eyes" and to inspire others to see with theirs, that made Nobby such a provocative and yet not quite conventionally helpful reader of one's work.
He read with the utmost seriousness—seeing in one's text its own peculiar lineage and trajectory, but extending its argument in directions he had found in pursuit of those he had placed in his own "pantheon."

In this, Nobby taught what it meant to invest one's thought with the deepest, most knowing, and most feelingful aspects of self.

There are three gestures that I associate with Nobby—three gestures that speak of the complex man that he was for me.
One was a gesture of Man Thinking;
the second—a gesture of Man Teaching;
the third—the gesture of the thrilled, barely self-contained child:
this was the gesture that brought light into darkness: play into reflection; the libidinal into thought.

In the last months of Nobby's life—the man became,

most of all, a version of that intensely present, libidinally invested child.
I was not adequate to follow him into that place—
Memories of the thinker and the teacher were too important to me—
I feared their loss and their compromise.
But I paid the price with loss of another kind.

Now, I am able to see those three gestures together again—
to glean their combined meaning:
to feel the awe, the puzzlement, the intense pleasure and—dare I say it—the love, that will always be associated for me—with Nobby.

Hayden White

I have a friend who works on presence, more particularly the difference between presence and meaning. He points out that we moderns have tended to overvalue meaning at the expense of presence. We are not content to be, we must also mean.

But a poem does not mean. It is. It is presence.

I think that this can be said of Norman O. Brown. Nobby was pure presence. And remains so.

Nobby did not believe, of course, in the resurrection of the flesh, or did he? ("Oh, Lord, I believe. Help Thou my unbelief.")

The real presence. "Here is my body. Take and eat."

Queer Jesus. Queer Nobby.
Presence is perversion. To be there is perverse. Nobby was there and therefore now is here.

To be there is perversion. The question is not "To be or not to be" but how to be there.

The way Nobby celebrated poetry is legendary, but it is also scandalous, even perverse.

"There is only poetry," he said. Is this statement to be taken literally or figuratively? "Only poetry is there." "There is only poetry." If there is no there there, there is no poetry there.

Of course, it is very, very difficult to be there. Very difficult to be present, to be a presence. You have to work at it all the time, even to the point of burning up the ego. Nobby worked at it all the time.

I like to remember Nobby in his last years, even as he was burning out the last "unlived lines" of his robust body.

We came upon him one day,
head on hands on table,
oblivious of all.

He started up
And fixed us with his Panic eye
Grasping at his nurse
Till Beth settled him
Like a sage ostler used to gentling skittish horses

In the alcove he sat with us,
Like an obedient child
Trying to remember
What it had never learned,
Under our dumb interrogation

Jerry Neu remarked the other day on Nobby's power, even after he had lost his memory and most of his ability to speak, to give the gift of presencing as when, for an instant the last time we saw him, he fixed you in a glance of fierce joy and smiled and touched you and said, as he said to us, a number of times that day: "again, again, again."

I liked being in Nobby's presence. It always seemed

an honor and a privilege. You knew that he was working—working at being there—and I for one, when I had the honor of being with him—always felt that I was intruding upon a very sacred labor—the all but impossible labor of being there.

Carl E. Schorske

Nobby came into my life sixty years ago in the Office of Strategic Services, wartime predecessor of the CIA. The Army, in its infinite wisdom, had created a kind of holding tank for recruits of exceptional skills or unusual knowledge whom it could not fit easily into its normal functional formations. It was called the "Overqualified Pool." From that pool, the OSS fished out Nobby. In no time, he became an expert in French politics and culture—especially that of the Resistance.

For me and others who came to know him in the OSS, Nobby remained forever after "the overqualified man." Throughout his intellectual development, he brought to bear the superabundance of his ever-expanding erudition to enrich, transform and transcend his ideas. He enthusiastically imparted them to others in writing, the classroom—even on picnics and on memorable walks.

Our friendship was intensely intellectual. He liked Augustine's phrase "Amor intellecualis," and that is what we had. He was now my teacher, now my companion in exploration, now my critic—a critic who, even when I resisted, shook me out of my dogmatic slumbers. As educator, Nobby worked with the Nietzschean injunction: "Become what you are!" He utilized his own learning to shake you up, not so much to convert you to his own always strong views, but to press you to transform yourself, to urge you to self-transcendence.

At Wesleyan our friendship ripened and deepened, with a shared political orientation as an important bond. We worked on Henry Wallace's campaign together. Nobby, a more committed Marxist than I, also had the stronger poetic sensibility. He wanted to explore the problem of alienation through studying the romantics. Shelley and Keats were his favorites at the time, the one for his resistance to political reaction and his sense of justice, the other for his psychological insight. Shelley's *Prometheus Bound* particularly gripped Nobby, with its defiance of divine power even in defeat. One of its closing verses appears often in Nobby's later writing, premonitory as it was of his own disillusionment with history and its promise of realizing a utopian political vision: "To hope till hope creates from its own wreck the thing it contemplates...."

....Beth will remember too how we listened together to a musical favorite of hers and Nobby's, Brahms' *Alto Rhapsody*. That work and its recording spoke to the Marxist intellectual: Goethe's verse celebrated the alienated wanderer in a frozen world. Brahms' romantic-classical setting captured the poignancy of the text. Last not least, the soloist was Marian Anderson—the glorious black contralto who had been denied the right to sing in Constitution Hall, by its owners, the Daughters of the American Revolution. The combination of art and politics produced a powerfully moving experience.... Nobby, deeply poetic though he was, always resonated best with works of art that comported well with his philosophic vision. In his last post-systemic and symbolist phase, poetry often posed the questions, took priority. But the poetic materials always were part of his larger, ceaseless philosophic quest.

Where Nobby's outlook underwent its most drastic change at the end of the Wesleyan years was, I believe, in his abandonment of hope—or faith—in history. Not just in Progress, but in history as a mode of making meaning of human experience. This is not the place to trace the brilliant trajectory of his development in that regard, from the turn from Marx to Freud, then on to poetry and the exploration of symbols, to the final, almost frantic para-religious search for a world that could be unified in its irreducible multiplicity through the laws of chaos or the structure of chance. Midway in that quest fell Nobby's reckoning with history in a book based on Vico and Joyce. The title says it all: *Closing Time*. It is at once the pub-keepers signal that the bar is closing, that the fun is over; but also an affirmation, that history is cyclical, an endless round that only repeats what mankind has experienced before, that it goes nowhere. In Plato's words, "Time is the moving image of eternity."

Here in Santa Cruz in 1981 Nobby and I taught a seminar together on Goethe's *Faust*. It was something we had wanted to do in our Wesleyan years, a project realizable at last after I retired. It turned out to be a wonderful sparring match, between the champions of historical and philosophic visions. I sought meaning in Faust's changing projects and their historical relatedness, even as failed quests;

Nobby focussed on the explosions and the unleashing of the terrors which make of history the story of wrecks confusedly hurled in the endless round of life and death. He gave me not only a run for my money, but the time of my life. The seminar, with the walks on which we framed our strategies for it, was just a peak in a lifetime of endless conversation with the most original, stimulating person I ever knew. Now it's Closing Time. The words are hard to speak.

Rebecca Herzig

Norman O. Brown was in his eightieth year when I met him, wispy and wrinkled. I was in my twentieth, broad-shouldered and pink-cheeked. Despite appearances, it was not clear to either of us who would predecease whom. A shared preoccupation with the grave gave birth to our conversations.

At the time, my primary hope was to make a quiet exit from this wretched, violent world. This aim did not appear to unnerve the man I called Mr. Brown. Instead, it drew his curiosity. He engaged me about death and self-destruction, inquired about it when I moved on to other subjects. ("I'm sorry for poking," he once said after asking yet again what I thought about suicide, "You notice I do that.") Mr. Brown was welcoming me to join him in thinking, in unflinching thinking. He enrolled me in an ongoing discussion with the dead: Blake and Nietzsche,

Bataille and Freud. That is to say, he conducted my absorption in death to the life of the mind, and hence, conducted my attention to life.

This made the world habitable.

This is not to say he offered redemption. He had, as he put it one afternoon, "outlived the need for redemption." His method of assisting a desolate girl, a most unusual method, was to walk her even further into the abyss. At the close of our first meeting, Mr. Brown handed me a slip of paper on which he'd scrawled the word *LIEBESTOD* in red ink, a call to contemplate the inseparability of love and death. No promises of peaceful resolution. Certainly no assurance of the steady hand of an omniscient Father. In place of my petulant search for justice, in lieu of dreams of reason and order, he illuminated the path of madness, squander, and exuberant excess. Not *justitia*, but *amor*.

Instead of God, Chance.

Chance afforded levity, merriment. Even, or perhaps especially, with respect to death. On one of our walks, Mr. Brown encountered a colleague who asked what he'd been doing lately. "Just dying," Mr. Brown replied. The colleague gaped and sputtered apologetically. "Oh, don't worry," Mr. Brown cheerfully corrected. "There's nothing to it. Easy as falling off a log." He continually punctured my youthful solemnity, prodding until I laughed despite myself. On one autumnal walk, he plucked a gigantic leaf from our path and studied its brown and curled edges. "Like you," he teased affectionately, "prematurely withered!"

Chance also afforded a sense of possibility, of genuine newness. For Chance meant nothing was safe. (On one blustery day, Mrs. Brown kindly advised us to be careful as we headed out for a walk in the woods. "Wary of what?" Mr. Brown asked. "Falling trees or our own suicidal impulses?") Chance meant nothing was safe—ultimately, all is expendable, all is expended. Nothing, not even painstakingly hoarded loneliness, could be protected. But nothing, not even the most treasured friendship, would be spared.

Jay Cantor

In the obituary for Nobby in the *New York Times* his college roommate Stuart Hampshire called him "a victim of theories." That rankled. It made me remember an ordinary phrase Nobby often used, and always with more than ordinary force: "But that's not it." In fact Nobby once gave a lecture with that title—about his own work, naturally, meaning, that is to say that *he* hadn't gotten something right. Nobby always took what I thought was an unnatural glee in savaging his own work. And, unlike me, he was mostly indifferent when others criticized him, probably because he had already shed the skin they tried to bite, already unsaid what he had once said.

But that's not it. The "it" might be some point that needed revising in his reading of William Carlos Williams or of Joyce. Or St. Augustine. Or Locke. But really the it—the big It—that had to be retold was, to put it grandly—and I hope accurately—what the world needed to overcome the world's divisions, its *mine or thine*. That divisiveness was the Fall itself, said Gerrard Winstanley, the founder of the Diggers in 1650. Winstanley, with his fantasy of a free and sharing community, was undoubtedly a victim of theories, too.

"Many people discovered the unconscious before me, but I married it," Freud said. So like Nobby, or Winstanley, Freud was the victim of a theory. But I don't think there's an alternative. You may wager or just stand around the table, but standing around requires a theory, too; one that believes—wrongly, I think—that isolation, separation, is possible. And those bachelors aren't, I think, the people we remember.

But no, that's not it, either. Nobby, remarkably enough wasn't the man who didn't wager, but he wasn't the victim of a theory either. Or not just one theory. Oh, like Freud he married them, right enough, but when it came to theory he was something of a serial monogamist. I remember a month when I heard him say on different days that we were "all Maoists," or all "Muslims," or all "followers of John Cage."

But then N. O. Brown himself, I mean who was he when he's at home? Well, he showed himself in the motion, of course—in the same way you might play a game of connect the dots and at the end have a picture of a face. A puckish one, in this case, with darting but very observant eyes.

His method reminds me of a tick in his conversation, that he'd so often begin a sentence with *That is to say*. That is to say, you start out with something from Freud, but that's not it, so you have to revise it, showing how it's like an aphorism of Nietzsche's, that is to say it has this facet that's like a line in Charles Olson. So *that is to say* is the original fiat, as Nietzsche wrote somewhere, the *this is that* that forges links between realms once thought disparate, once thought mine or thine; that makes the connection that allows the current to flow, the filament to glow. Eros, that is to say, makes connections that show Eros—with a puckish face, probably, and maybe cloven feet.

That is to say, Nobby wasn't the victim of a singular theory, far from it; but he did have a singular theme, connection itself, love, the true Penelope to which this Ulysses remained always faithful. Love was the energy of his motion and the goal of his activity, showing desire even as he spoke about desire.

But that's not it, either. Nobby wasn't the victim of a theory *or* of a theme. He was the victim rather—and it was a fortunate fall—of a mission. He wrote in the introduction to *Life Against Death* that he had inherited "from the Protestant tradition a conscience which insisted that intellectual work should be directed toward the relief of man's estate." *That is to say*, Nobby—if you knew him, I think you already know this about him—had a calling. Love calling him to save us from the Fall into mine and thine by means of love.

A calling is a driven urgent, inescapable slavery. No wonder he wanted to be free of that burden—and so he would dive into the labor of the negative and enjoy the momentary freedom of the corrosive. But the dive into *but that's not it* always revealed itself as another aspect of the calling he had tried, like Jonah, to escape. The negative became a force to refine and change and shape the words he would use next, helped him rediscover his themes again, new words for old.

That is to say, rebirth was always another of Nobby's themes. Resurrection of the body; and the apocalypse of divisions between bodies; until we achieved the longed for unity: Love's Body. But as Hampshire says, in a way that's both very true and very blind, an unrepressed life, was 'not really his life or anybody's life.' In this, I'd wager, Nobby's apocalypse, his paradise, is no different from the aphorisms of Blake's *Marriage of Heaven and Hell*, or Nietzsche's *Zarathustra*, or, and especially, the Gospels—all of which are invaluable, though not precisely anyone's life. Not yet, and perhaps not ever. But clearly there are sublimities that allow us to see our world now more clearly; and there are unattainable goals that produce a forward motion from idea to idea, from dot to dot—and that produced, in this case, Nobby's angular, surprising conjunctions, amazing sentences that are condensed like the best poetry, yet strangely lucid, too, words that will be forever an incitement to heal the world, to connect the dots, to connect the words, poem commenting on poem, one thought, one word, one world, leading to another, always dancing us forward.

But not just leading to *any* other word, mind you. Nobby didn't suffer foolish words, or foolish graduate students, gladly. I know because I was often the fool in question, sometimes making his round face nearly apoplectic with rage. But the point wasn't the pleasure of chastising or embarrassing me—or not just that anyway, the point was the calling, the task, *the work*. Sometimes I would think myself to be walking with him by the ocean, and find he had stopped several steps back and just gone off in a different direction, left me to blather to the air. Then, when I came to my senses, I could rejoin him, thinking still, still busy about the work—but happy enough when company showed up.

Now he's gone off again, and I wish to God I knew how I might run to catch up.

Stephen Brown

I want first to express, on behalf of our family, how marvellous it is that this gathering could be arranged, and that all of you could attend. We know that many of you have come some distance; we thank each of you for your presence. We are very aware of, and very thankful for, the special efforts of a number of individuals—Jerry Neu of course, but many others—directed to making sure that, as a family, we had this opportunity to share our experience, and to process our memories.

When I say "as a family", I am of course thinking of members present: our Mother especially, my brother Tom, his daughter Meika, my sister Becky, and my sister Sukie, her husband Gary, their children Sara & Jeremy, and my wife Lilly and our children Alex & Lisa… And beyond: I'm thinking of family no longer with us, particularly of my father's beloved mother Margarita, and of his father Norman, and of his sister Eileen, and all those who, with my father, continue to live, as reflections, within the lives of us that remain.

Today, however, my sense of family really includes all of you gathered here. And that, for me, is itself an important point of closure. You see, my father's life, as I see it now, had multiple layers—each being its own enactment, its own reflection of his passion. He was a wonderful father, yet I had the sense as a child that the major part of who he was resided in a world largely outside my view. Now, I see that, having left his original family roots to become part of the newness of America, he sought refuge and grounding in a family life that was to be far safer, far more secure, than the world of ideas that was his preoccupation.

Our mother was a huge source of unquestioning love and support—for us, her children, but first-of-all for our father. I remember one day well, when my mother met me coming out of the house. She looked at me with a special glow in her face and proclaimed, "Now there's proof that your father is a great man!" Being a child, and therefore not requiring proof, I made some non-response to my mother, whereupon I was told that his book, I believe that it was *Life*

Against Death, had been accepted for publication. My mother's pride and excitement that day remain with me in my memory. *Our mother's immense strength and loyalty will inspire me as long as I live.*

Our father (I say this with honour and respect) was a *wild man*. His iconoclasm, his passionate sense of discovery, his curiosity about the unknown, found expression not only in the classroom, but also in our home. As children, we took unspoken lessons from him in balancing civility and outrageous rebellion. One childish memory that I have was an odd preparation, involving a few colleagues, prior to an evening for which I knew I was to be made absent. They were doing some clumsy construction of a number of shallow tubs. My father was not speaking about what they were for, but a sympathetic colleague took me aside and told me that they would be used for grape crushing, "Using bare feet," he said with a grin. Whatever the Bacchanalian outcome, the exchange gave me an early impression of the lure of the forbidden.

Another childhood memory that I honour him for, is his sense of beauty, especially as reflected in the world of the outdoors. I remember well the hiking trips with him and my brother Tom, when we were both quite young. His love of walking the earth remains with me today.

His intellectual legacy is for all to celebrate. My relationship with him was that of father-and-son, with all the complexities that we are aware of. He was my model and my rival; my tyrant and my saint. And I want to say that I have a great sense of gifting, that he was my father. I loved him passionately.

And Now I'm saying to you: he is free, and he is in flight. No pain; no earthly bond. In his final stages, having first released his mind from servitude, he lived a simple life. His family was with him and his attendants cherished him. They approached me once, wanting me to know that my father was an angel. "You know," one of them said earnestly, "your father is a very happy man."

I believe now that he is.